And I Call Him ...
"Father"

Kitty Clymer

CROSSBOOKS
PUBLISHING

CrossBooks™
A Division of LifeWay
1663 Liberty Drive
Bloomington, IN 47403
www.crossbooks.com
Phone: 1-866-879-0502

First published by CrossBooks 9/3/2010

ISBN: 978-1-6150-7295-8 (sc)
ISBN: 978-1-6150-7296-5 (dj)
Library of Congress Control Number: 2010936319

Printed in the United States of America
This book is printed on acid-free paper.

PREFACE

And I Call Him..."Father" is selected excerpts from inspired writings from thirty years of journalling during times of seeking God's guidance, His voice, His word, His will, and His presence. He draws near to us when we draw near to Him.

This book is intended to bring you blessing; to speak to you when you cannot hear; to bring encouragement; to bring you moments with God; to help usher you into His presence; and to inspire you to daily quiet times resulting in a deeper walk.

You can read this book cover to cover, digesting it slowly for inspiration, or you can open it randomly and meditate on a special selection for your day. No inspirational writings could ever take the place of the one-true inspired written Word of God, but it is my hope that sharing these pages from my journals will encourage you in your own path of quiet times and journalling.

I like to open this little book randomly, or think of a page number, and turn to that page as inspiration for the day. Many hours of searching, seeking, and listening from my own personal journals are being poured forth to share with you.

My prayer is that this book will enrich your walk with God, encourage you in times of need, and help keep your feet moving toward the mark of your highest calling. Mostly, I hope it encourages *you* to take that daily time, to listen, and to journal your very own inspirations as He comes to *you* through His written holy word, the Bible.

DEDICATION

To You, Father, I dedicate this book, for Your endless love and inspiration, and to all who seek to hear Your voice and draw nearer to You.

May these recorded journal inspirations and Your written holy word (the Bible) inspire us, bringing us "up hither" to greater heights with You.

My heart belongs to You, Father...
like the melody belongs to the song...
like the blooms belong to the spring...
like the blue belongs to the skies...
like the waves belongs to the ocean....

As a bear dwells in a cave;
as a bee in a hive;
as the water in the seas;
as the sun in the sky;
I dwell in You.

Oh, how I love You.

Thank You for your daily inspiration, and if this little book can be any encouragement to even one other person to spend time alone with You, reading Your Word and journalling, to you alone, Father, I give You thanks, appreciation and praise!

Daily bread for your daily journey.

Words of inspiration

to steady your feet along the way....

knowing

quiet time

alone

with

Him

is the answer.

This little book is in honor of
and dedicated to
my Father...
The one who has made, not only this book, but, all things possible.

Father, I love You.
There is truly no one else like You.
Because You are mindful of us, O Father, I thank You and love You!

And...

To Mary,
my dearest earthly inspiration; my best friend for my whole life... the push when I need it...my Joseph, interpreting my dreams, and believing in me and keeping me hopeful.

To Jack,
my brother in life and my brother in spiritual matters;
the one who has called me "God-lover"
through every single experience of life
as he looked beyond my circumstances and saw my heart.

To Andrea,
my beautiful, godly sister-in-love,
who joined my brother, Jack, in my times of discouragement and seeking to steadily and lovingly encourage me toward God and the inerrancy of His word.

To my Mom,
who, like Father God, never stops loving me.

To Lee,
because his tenacious love for writing rekindled my own pursuit to finish this little book begun in 1993.

To Marion,
my friend who joined me on my path in 2006, and "swooshed" with amazing spiritual growth when she stepped on the journey, and never stops asking to read my writings.

And to You, dear reader of this book,
that you, too, will be "swooshed" away with the "presence"...
the very tangible, amazing presence of God.
It is He who wants to *lavish* His love on you
and take you to higher ground,
as you begin or continue your own daily devotional times
and journalling with
God's word.

I love you so -- each of you.

Thank you for who you are in my life.

A PRAYER

Father God,

Prepare us.

Consecrate us.

Thank you for plowing up fallow ground in our hearts and lives for something spectacular! Help us, Lord, to grasp this!

You have been amazing and astonishing to us. Forgive any doubts and help us see You as You look into our eyes and tell us who we are and who You would have us become.

Oh, Father, we ask for none other than an amazing voyage steered by the rudder of your Word and presence and fueled by Your love. We ask for favorable winds to bring us through the deep waters of our souls, to help us discover the treasures of the wisdom of abiding in You, and to take us to new places in Your love and in your Word, both with You, and with others. Chart our course, Father. Be the Captain of our life's ship!

We so love You, Father, and we are taken with Your presence and our communion together! Capture our hearts and minds once again, with each new day's dawning.

Come, Lord, let "us" be. We are willing to follow You, for You said, "Come, follow me, and I will make you fishers of men." You will make us, fashioning us after Your love so that we might be Your radiant love to others and to our very own selves. We desire to discover who You are and who we are in You.

We ask You, Lord, to speak to us in words, thoughts, and images we can understand, and we thank You. Let us accurately discern Your perfect will and have the right responses to You. Let us hear Your voice, not that of our own, and follow You accordingly, regardless of our own desires and wants. Let us see You, hear You, and feel Your presence.

Open our eyes and ears to see and hear clearly.

You alone are God, and we welcome You in our place. We lay aside our desires. We lay aside our fears. We want Your perfect will, for You are the Holy One, the God of the Universe, the father of Abraham, the Magnificent One, our Savior, our Master, our Teacher, our Counselor, our Friend, our Guide, our Beloved! You are the One we seek!

Thank you, Father, for Your indescribable love and presence. Overcome us with Your Will. We will follow. We will wait. We will go. We will sit in Your presence until we hear Your voice saying, "Go this way."

Thy will be done. You, Father, are our complete desire.

The God who sees knows

"You keep track of all my sorrows. You have collected all my tears in Your bottle. You have recorded each one in Your book."
Psalm 56:8 NLT

Each tear collected,
as it rolled down your cheek …
or as it silently drenched your heart.

Each tear …
He saw it.
He captured it,
and saved it in a bottle.

And now,
He uses it … to refresh you;
to drench you
with blessing,
with healing
and recovery
from the wounded past …
flowing
to a better future …
a better now.

Float on the tears of your past
which are now becoming
rivers of pathway
to your present.

Listen as He whispers.

"After the earthquake, a fire, but the Lord was not in the fire; and after the fire, there was a sound of a gentle whisper."
1 Kings 19:12 NLT

You speak from the mighty waters, Lord.
You speak through the silence.
You speak in the darkness of the night.
You speak in the rising of the sun.

Great is our God, and greatly to be praised.
You alone make all things right.
There is no turning back in You,
for you have steadfastly held our hands,
even when our hearts have been prone to wander.

You alone are the great God. The I AM.

You are, You were, and You ever shall be.

How magnificent is Your name, Lord Jehovah, the Holy One of Israel.

Your voice can be heard in many ways, but I thank you most for the still small voice...the gentle whisper. Quieten my mind and heart at this very moment, Lord, so that I may hear you speak.

Loving the one whom we have not seen...

Jesus said to Thomas, "Because you have seen me Thomas, do you now believe (trust, have faith)? Blessed and happy and to be envied are those who have never seen Me, and yet have believed and adhered to and trusted in and relied in Me."

John 20:29 AMP

Look at the trees as they gently flow in the breeze. The breeze you cannot see, but you can see the *result* of that unseen force.

Put a new balloon not yet filled to your mouth and gently blow, and you see the balloon begin to take shape and grow.

Just like God, though we cannot see His presence, we can certainly see the results of and feel that breeze. We *know* He is there.

Trust, believe, have faith in God, for as surely as the gentle breezes rock the treetops, His presence is evidenced in our lives by His gentle leading and great love.

Trust. Believe today. Expect His presence. Recognize His presence.

Be still, and *know* that He is God. Blessed and happy and to be envied are those who have never seen Him, yet believe, trust in, and rely on Him!

Deep calls unto deep.

"Deep calls to deep at the sound of Your waterfalls; all Your breakers and Your waves have rolled over me. The Lord will command His lovingkindness in the daytime; and His song will be with me in the night. A prayer to the God of my life."

Psalm 42:7, 8 NAS

Deep calls unto deep, so His word is calling to you. Know that He desires the deepest places of your heart, your soul, and your mind. He wants to speak to you in that deep place.

Let your mind not *wander* to unfamiliar places that cause you to *wonder* or doubt Him. Hold steadfastly to your love for Him.

Keep loving Him unashamedly. Quieten your mind and spend time with Him.

You can be as Enoch as you keep seeking His presence and be "caught up" in Him. "Come up hither." That is where you want to abide. Make efforts to move toward spiritual awareness, not toward fulfilling the wants of your personality.

Enter into this day with a greater awareness of His Presence. Be conscious of Him.

See yourself as He sees you. Open your arms wide as He fills you with treasures of love, truth, peace, joy, laughter, and happiness.

Surely deep calls unto deep. From the depths of your heart, cry out to Him, and from the depths of His love, He will respond.

Perceiving thoughts as Jesus did

"Jesus knew what they were thinking and asked, 'Why are you thinking these things in your hearts?'"

Luke 5:22 NAS

Jesus perceived thoughts and answered them aloud. How powerful would it be if we were so "in tune" that we could hear thoughts and needs of others? How could it change the lives of others if we were able to respond to their very thoughts?

Luke 5:17-23 is the story of the friends who carried a paralyzed man on a stretcher to Jesus. The scribes and Pharisees began to "reason" in their minds about this sight, and Jesus' words, "Friend, your sins have been forgiven you." Jesus "perceived" the thoughts of the scribes and Pharisees, and answered their thoughts aloud.

Jesus perceives your thoughts today. "Child, your sins are forgiven you." Therefore, rise, be healed, and go on your way rejoicing! Walk in your forgiveness. Forgive yourself as God has forgiven you. Be paralyzed no more with the weight of guilt and shame which so easily beset you, keeping you from being all that you can be. Walk as if that sin had never touched your life.

You are forgiven, and as Jesus perceives thoughts, He has spoken to your thoughts, your mind, your needs and provided an answer: "Your sins are forgiven you."

Truth

"I am the way, the truth, and the life."

John 14:6 KJV

Darkness cannot hide the face of God,
for truth arrives on the wings of angels…
on the tongues of men

selected

by God

to know …
to know Him well …
who seek,
who ask,
who knock,
who find.

Life's passion is to know the truth.

For He is the truth. The only truth.

So, how can you comprehend the love of God?

Nature is only a taste,
a touch,
a display…
on the edges.

Greater heights await you; greater depths, as deep calls unto deep. Higher, deeper, experiencing His love. It is yours for the asking.

"I am the Way, the Truth, and the Life."

Truth brings freedom.

"You will know the truth, and the truth will make you free."
John 8:32 NIV

The wisdom of God
is not in the presence or pleasures of man,
but in the depths of your soul.
For out of the soul
comes forth
the histories of wisdom.

Wisdom is cumulative.
It is there for you to draw upon.

There is certainly no new thing on the earth. Solomon was right about wisdom.

Listen to the Psalms; the songs; the wisdom from the written word of God. Flowing freely...to you...for the asking...for the taking.

Relax, and let Him take the reigns of your life. Don't try to figure it all out. Walk in expectation and joy. Freely flow. Freely Go. Freely live. Freely love.

You are free because of truth.

He is your dwelling place.

"Be still, and know that I am God."

Psalms 46:10 NIV

Come. Sit together...and talk....and love...for hours. Are you willing?

You know there is no other place like this. This is ecstasy. You are His.... so His.

He shares His secret place with you. You come together, here, this place to exchange your love. You are always welcome.

It is His place. You are His place. He dwells with and within you.

Then...go forth. Be His presence to others.

He so loves you.

Be still, and know that He is God.

There is no darkness in God.

> *"God is light, and in Him there is no darkness at all."*
> *I John 1:5 NAS*

God's presence.

This is the presence He wants us to walk in. Powerful. Peaceful. Abiding presence.

Quietly listen. Rest. Heal. Love. Experience His agape love.

Free to flow, and free to go to places yet known. He is in all places. Just recognize His presence. He is with you. Peace, love, and joy come from within. He is within. He is "I AM."

Look up, my child, what do you see?
    A weathered vessel? Or His presence?
Rest your face as the sun bathes your skin.
    He whispers peace and joy from deep within.

Yes, be anxious for nothing,
    for you will truly see,
your life can be in His presence.
    You can depend on Him.

He loves you. Don't you know?
    Don't you *know*?
Take His presence with you.
    Take His peace everywhere you go.

Free to live. Free to love.

Fear released. Love truly, as they say, you have never loved before. Love deeply from the wells within. He chooses to speak to you, just as He chose to speak to the woman at the well. Do you think anything can change that path? No, you have tasted of the living water and it springs from within. You will truly thirst no more. He has arrived at the well to speak to you. He is the well from which you draw your strength, peace, joy, and love. Drink in. Immerse yourself. Total immersion.

There can be no darkness, for He is the light. Bask and breathe and meditate on His peace and love. Enter in.

He says, “Fret no more!” Your life is in His hands. He is at the helm.
He is light, and in Him there is no darkness.

Dwell in the secret place.

"He that dwelleth in the secret place of the Most High, shall abide under the shadow of the Almighty."

Psalms 91:1 KJV

This is His place, the secret place. This is your place to share with Him --- to see the demonstration of His love and His voice.

Consider the beach. Do you not run to see the rising of the morning sun? You take your camera. You wait, for the perfect moment, and you see the sun rising in all its splendor.

It is just like that with God. Will you run to Him? As excited as the opportunity to see the sun rise? Come! Come with joy and expectation! Bring the "camera" of your soul, and you will see and witness amazing things.

And stay. Stay long enough to see the heavens split open with the first rays of morning light. Stay long enough to get the full view; to experience what you need to take you through the remainder of the day.

The sunrise is in your home, your porch, your office --- any place where you will take time to spend with Him. It is not necessarily a literal physical thing, for we speak in spiritual terms.

The "sunrise" is *the place you have daily* ***purposed*** *time with Him.* Let the written word arise and bring new light, new encouragement to your day... every day. Take time to allow His word to be your sunrise...and bring the "camera" of your soul.

It is new and fresh every morning. There are no two mornings exactly the same. Remember. He awaits for you every day wanting to share "sunrise" (your "purposed" time) whether at actual sunrise, mid-day or evening. Find that place and time to "dwell" in the secret place.

Know Him in spirit and in truth.

"True worshipers will worship the Father in spirit and in truth."
John 4:23 NIV

God's way is hidden from those who seek to walk in their own understanding....who seek to understand and place God in "scientific" understanding. God is spirit, and those who worship Him, those who *know* Him, must know Him in spirit.

You will not *know* God on a merely intellectual level. It is a heart thing. Knowing God flows from the deepest part of your heart, your inner man, the one within. Each and every man, woman, and child has within him/her an innate knowing of and longing for God. "For since the creation of the world, His invisible attributes, His eternal power and divine nature, have been clearly seen, being understood through what has been made so that they are without excuse." Romans 1:20 NIV

God does not dwell in your brain. God knows no formulas; He has no "steps." He is known innately by all of creation.

We can taste and see what is altogether good -- what is altogether God. Beyond reasoning is that place....a place of peace, and power and love... not deciphered by codes or knowledge of this world's systems --- the place where deep calls unto deep.

You can *know* God in spirit and in truth.

Wait...but never give up!

> *"...from the first day that you set your heart on understanding and on humbling yourself before your God, your words were heard, and I have come in response to your words."*
>
> *Daniel 10:12 NAS*

Daniel mourned and prayed for three entire weeks. On the twenty-fourth day, he saw a man in a vision, while the men who were with him did not see. Daniel heard the man in the vision say, "O Daniel....I have now been sent to you...for from the first day that you set your heart on understanding this and on humbling yourself before your God, your words were heard, and I have come in response to your words. But the prince of the kingdom of Persia was withstanding me for twenty-one days; then behold, Michael, one of the chief princes, came to help me." Daniel 10:12-13 NAS

I repeat: And the man in the vision said, "I have come in response to your words."

Sometimes it takes "twenty-one days" for a prayer to get through principalities and powers, but response to prayer *will* come. In fact, *a response is initiated the moment the prayer leaves your lips*; the moment your breath forms words of request.

Consider the person who runs out of gas on the interstate. He/she contacts by phone someone to come and assist. From the moment the call is received, the hearer is "on the way" with the answer. It may take five minutes, twenty minutes, or hours, depending on the situation.

Don't give up. Don't despair. Don't think for one moment that God has not seen your cries and that He will not answer you. For He will. Sometimes the "principalities and powers" are so strong against our prayers, there is great hindrance in seeing the answer.

But the answer always comes. Don't quit believing. Don't give up.

"From the first day that you set your heart on understanding and on humbling yourself before God, your words were heard."

Give me eyes to see and ears to hear.

"Some of the people, therefore, when they heard these words, were saying, 'This certainly is the Prophet.' Others were saying, 'This is the Christ.' Still others were saying, 'Surely the Christ is not going to come from Galilee, is He?'.....So a division occurred in the crowd because of Him."

John 7:40. 41.43 NAS

Father,

Today I need clarity. Give me eyes to see and ears to hear your perfect will for my life. The scripture is clear that some stood in His midst but did not know who Jesus was. Some even heard Jesus speak, but could not understand what he was saying.

I ask you, Father, to give me clear understanding of His words, Your Word, and clarity for my own life. Give me ears to hear, eyes to see, and a receptive heart that I might not "miss" Your presence.

Let me be acutely aware today of Your voice, Your way, and Your presence.

Loving like Jesus

> *"Peter said to Him (Jesus), 'Lord, why can I not follow You right now? I will lay down my life for you.' Jesus answered, 'Will you lay down your life for Me? Truly, truly, I say to you, a rooster will not crow until you deny Me three times.'"*
>
> *John 13:37 NAS*

Peter believed with all his heart he would lay down his life because of his love for Jesus. He said it. Peter said, "I will lay down my life for you." But his words did not line up with his actions. Three times the opportunity came for Peter to proclaim his love for Christ. He failed. His actions did not line up with his words. Perhaps fear of self-protection kept Peter from confessing three times his love for Jesus.

But we must focus on Jesus. In His humanness, was Jesus heartbroken over this betrayal? I would think so, for He was human as we, and suffered all things so that He might *know* how we feel. But He continued to love Peter, and Peter became "the rock" in Christianity.

Today, if we can hear His voice, and imitate His actions and His love, we can love those who say one thing, proclaiming their love, but their actions deny it. Because betrayal was a part of our Savior's life, when we, like Christ, are faced with betrayal, we have a Savior who knows and understands our pain.

How great a God we have that He would include in His word this heartbreaking story of betrayal, so when betrayal comes upon us, we would not consider it "strange," but would take comfort in the love of a Savior who has experienced all things as we. He knows. He sees. Take comfort.

We must realize the frailty and inconsistency of mere man, for we too, are merely human. All have fallen short of the glory of God.

Look unto Jesus, the author and finisher of our faith. He *will* keep His word. He *did* lay down His life for us. Let us love like Jesus loves..... knowing.....but loving anyway. He is the truth.

Father: I release the anger of unkept promises of love; untrue words; blinded love; love based in fear. I thank you that you understand all things I experience. You have borne my pain and carried my grief because you submitted to human experiences. You are a Savior who is touched by our pain, because you, too, have suffered this pain.

I submit my heart and my will unto the cross. I lay my disappointment at your feet, and I ask for the ability to love like Jesus not based on men's words and actions, but based on YOUR agape love. I forgive, because I, too, have been forgiven.

Thank you, Precious Savior.

The one true counselor

"Nevertheless I am continually with You;
You have taken hold of my right hand.
With Your counsel You will guide me
and afterward receive me to glory.
Whom have I in heaven but you?
And besides You, I desire nothing on earth.
My flesh and my heart may fail,
but God is the strength of my heart and my portion forever."
Psalm 73:23-26 NAS

There is no counsel like God's. Only He can speak the complete truth into your life. His word is His *word.* Read His written word to receive the counsel you need. Others may encourage and strengthen, but only God knows the future of your life -- the very plans and purposes He has for you.

The word of God drowns out the voice of men. The voice of man drowns out the voice of God.

Listen for the voice of God. Let the voice of men comfort and encourage, but the voice of God is the voice that brings direction, deliverance, unfailing love, and truth. Desire nothing on earth more than God; His voice; His word; His holding your right hand. He *will* lead you through.

He is the one true counsellor, our strength, and our portion.

Oh Father,
Besides you, I desire nothing on earth. Though my flesh and my heart may fail, you alone, O Father, are the strength of my life, my heart, and my portion forever. Nothing compares to being in your presence; to you; to your love. Thank you, Father.

A special prayer for today

“Sprinkle clean water on me, and I will be clean; cleanse me from all my filthiness and from all idols. Give me a new heart and put a new spirit within me; remove the heart of stone from my flesh and give me a heart of flesh. Put your Spirit within me and cause me to walk in Your statues, and I will be careful to observe your ordinances.”

(Rephrased from Ezekiel 36: 25-27 and formed into a prayer for this day.)

Write down this verse and carry it with you today. Read it every chance you get.

(Using God’s word formed into a prayer from your own lips is always a good thing.)

Wait is an action verb.

"I will stand like a guard to watch and place myself at the tower.
I will wait to see what He will say to me;
I will wait to learn how God will answer...."

Habakkuk 2:1 NCV

Relax, and let God take the reins of your life.

Don't try to figure it all out.

Just stand. And watch. Wait. He will answer.

Waiting is an action verb: anticipating,
knowing,
expecting.

That's the kind of waiting of which He speaks.

Know that He will answer.

Wait.

Choosing "the good part"

"...He entered a certain village; and a certain woman named Martha received Him into her house. And she had a sister called Mary, which also sat at Jesus' feet, and heard His word. But Martha was cumbered about much serving, and came to Him, and said, 'Lord do You not care that my sister has left me to serve alone? Bid her therefore that she help me.' And Jesus answered and said to her, 'Martha, Martha, you are careful and troubled about many things; But one thing is needful; and Mary has chosen that good part, which shall not be taken away from her.'"

Luke 11: 28-42 KJV

"One thing is needful; and Mary has chosen that good part."

There are always many things to be done. Have you ever completed a "to do" list?

The *urgent* cries out for your attention, when, in fact, the *important* things may be left unattended.

Do not let the *urgent* deny you what is really *important.*

Do not be cumbered about with service. Choose the good part --- the part that will never be taken away from you.

Sit at His feet.....today. Let go of the urgent, and do the *important* thing.

Father:
Though jobs, relationships, and all earthly activities can be taken away, I thank you for time at your feet, for this time is eternal and is truly the "good part" of life. I thank you that it is ok not to be "cumbered about", but sitting still...at your feet.

Come to the well of living water.

> *"If you knew the gift of God, and who it is who says to you, 'Give Me a drink,' you would have asked Him, and He would have given you living water."*
>
> *John 4:10 NIV*

Like a ship which is carried about on the water,
    I am carrying you.
Like a baby bird safe in its mother's nest,
    I am holding you.
Like an eagle soaring above the mountain tops,
    I am carefully keeping my eyes on you.
Like a newborn baby cradled for the very first time in its mother's arms,
    I am loving you.
Like the feast of a family's Thanksgiving table,
    I am feeding you.
Like the sun and the moon and the stars above,
    I am giving you light.
Like the lyrics of a famous writer/singer,
    I am singing words for soothing you.

Carrying, holding, watching, loving, feeding, giving you light, soothing you...through the Word.

Don't seek joy. Seek God. Joy comes from God, and He gives it to you from within. Nothing outside of Him can bring lasting joy. So seek not outward answers, but seek within.

Avoid strife, bitterness, and evil speaking. God never comes through those venues and that is not the way He speaks to us. He does not have to use harsh words with those who listen, who have a heart of love for Him and truly seek Him. Particularly you, for you truly want to hear and fellowship with Him. He sees your heart. Others cannot judge what they cannot see.

For man looks on the outward appearance, but God looks on the heart, and He sees *your* heart. Your actions may not always line up with your heart, but your heart steadies in times of quiet, and you return to the fountain of your joy.

You know there is a well that never runs dry, and coming daily keeps your heart, mind, and spirit drenched in peace and joy. So settle down. Settle in. And settle for nothing less than inner joy and peace. Let nothing steal that from you. Center on His love. Come to the inner sanctuary where God abides, untouchable by the world or the demands of others. Your hiding place. Your sanctuary....in Him.

Listen only to the voice of love. Remember: God is love. Love is God. Anything not said or done in love is not God.

Return to the fountain of joy....the well of living water. Drink of His water --the living water -- and you will thirst no more.

It's never too late.

"And one of the criminals who were hanged there was hurling abuse at Him, saying, 'Are you not the Christ? Save Yourself and us?' But the other answered, and rebuking him said, 'Do you not even fear God, since you are under the same sentence of condemnation? And we indeed are suffering justly, for we are receiving what we deserve for our deeds; but this man has done nothing wrong.' And he was saying, "Jesus, remember me when You come in Your kingdom?' And He said to him, "Truly I say to you, today you shall be with Me in Paradise."

Luke 23: 39-42 NAS

It's just that simple. Recognize your own sin; recognize who Jesus is; confess the holiness of Jesus, and make request unto Him. He hears. He answers.

How many times do you hear someone say, "It's too late."? It's never too late with Jesus. His mercy is never ending; unfailing; unfathomable.

It's just never too late with Jesus. No past is too dark. No path is too crooked. Today He wants to "be" with You in "paradise." And it is "paradise," in deed, being in His presence.

Be still.

Be still and know that I am God.

Psalm 46:10 NIV

Cease striving and know that I am God.

Psalm 46:10 NAS

For a lifetime, God has looked (carefully watched) over you. There is not one moment when you have escaped His loving eyes. He is a loving father gazing at His child, overwhelmed by how much one can love another. He loves you so much more than can be expressed in mere words.

Hesitate for a moment and breathe in His love. Let His love refresh….and sooth….and heal.

Be still in His love.

He says: "Do not be afraid." Overwhelmed by His presence? Know, just know, He has come to invade your thoughts, your chest, your heart. He wants to invade your life with His love. Not to worry: He is not the "Holy Police," watching for your faults, but He is the holy and *good father*, watching after and caring for you with eyes of love.

You will hear Him through the chirping of the birds; the wind rustling; the quiet moments; the silence. He speaks through His word and His creation.

Be silent.

Be still.

Let Him have fifteen minutes of uninterrupted time with you. No phone. No chatter. No interruptions. Just His written word.
Just fifteen quiet minutes. He calls *you* "child of God" – His child. Child... to the Most High God! What manner of love *is* this?

Dear precious Father, please quieten my mind.

I shall quieten my mind, as I listen for His voice.
I feel lost and afraid, so I have no choice.

How did I come to a place of "not hearing?"
How can I hear when I am constantly fearing?

Hush, mind! Be still. Fear, you cease..
He always comes to get me, for He is my peace.

He's love unconditional and love unfailing.
So I can stop this tempest and continual flailing.

I cannot encourage you, for I can't encourage me.
I feel as the prophet who sat under the tree.

Voices of confusion? Peace, be still.
Let the Master speak, for I know He will.

He's never let me down, and this won't be the first,
For I am standing at the well; for His presence I thirst.

Come now, Lord Jesus, I sit at your feet.
Free from the frenzy, the world's demanding street.

Breathe on me, oh, breath of God.
Let cool gentle winds rush over my soul to make me whole.

I have come to give you life, and life more abundantly.
Don't fret at your lack. Cast your eyes only on Me.

Don't stare at your sin, for your debt has been paid.
I am the I AM; to the world you're no slave.

Don't let swirling winds take your peace,
For upon hearing His voice, the winds cease.

Follow God.

"Now on the day that the tabernacle was erected the cloud covered the tabernacle, the tent of the testimony, and in the evening it was like the appearance of fire over the tabernacle, until morning. So it was continuously, the cloud would cover it by day and the appearance of fire by night. Whenever the cloud was lifted from over the tent, afterward the sons of Israel would then set out; and in the place where the cloud settled down, there the sons of Israel would camp. At the command of the Lord the sons of Israel would set out, and at the command of the Lord they would camp; as long as the cloud settled over the tabernacle, they remained camped. Even when the cloud lingered over the tabernacle for many days, the sons of Israel would keep the Lord's charge and not set out. If sometimes the cloud remained a few days over the tabernacle, according to the command of the Lord they remained camped. Then according to the command of the Lord they set out....Whether it was two days or a month or a year that the cloud lingered over the tabernacle, staying above it, the sons of Israel remained camped and did not set out, but when it was lifted, they did set out. At the command of the lord they set out; they kept the Lord's charge, according to the command of the Lord through Moses."

Numbers 9:15 -20, 22, 23 NAS

It's just that simple. Don't "go" without God's presence.

There's just no point in going without the Lord. That would be futile.

If God provided such obvious signs for the Israelites, He likewise, will be *sure* we *know* His direction. He *wants* us to *know* His will. He is not trying to hide His will from us.

Father: Open my eyes and let me see your perfect leading, for I know it is Your will that I follow after You only. I only want to "go" with your Presence. If it takes two days, I wait for your Presence. If it takes two weeks, or a month, or a year...I wait for Your Presence, Father, for I ONLY want to GO where you lead.

God, our great deliverer

> *"The children of Israel walked upon dry land in the midst of the sea; and the waters were a wall unto them on their right hand, and on their left."*
>
> *Exodus 14:22 KJV*

Seas part when we have reached our end, for God is there, always there, and we can walk over on dry ground.

Manna comes from heaven only in times of great hunger and great need. Burning bushes only happen in the desert/wilderness.

It is His delight to deliver us; to rescue us. So take heart when you've reached the edge of the sea or the desert with no water or food. That is when a "bush" can talk to you, the sea can open, and manna can come from heaven. For it is His will, His way to show Himself strong on our behalf.
It is our opportunity to see the hand of God in our lives at the edge of that sea. So we can actually welcome the edge of the sea; the empty pantry; and/or the desert experience. For then, we can see God in all His glory.

Trust Him.
At the bottom of the sea is a pathway for the redeemed to cross over.

Never cease to pray.

"Moreover as for me, God forbid that I should sin against the Lord in ceasing to pray for you: but I will teach you the good and right way: Only fear the Lord, and serve him in truth with all your heart; for consider how great things he hath done for you."

I Samuel 12:23 NAS

Even after the people demanded a king, Samuel did not cease praying for the perfect will of God for the people. God wanted personal relationship with the people; He wanted them to seek Him, not a king. He wanted people to want *Him*; to talk and fellowship with *Him*.

Samuel was committed to continue praying for the people, even when they were "off-track," and to live the life before them by "taking them by the hand and leading them in the right way."

Continue to live your life walking with God no matter what others may be doing. As you have heard it said, "Let your life speak." Your life is the most powerful tool outside of God's word in bringing others "along the way." Continue, like Samuel, to pray for the perfect will of God, and then, live your life before others in such a way as to teach them the good and right way, serving God with all your heart.

Choose my path, O Lord.

"The king's heart is in the hand of the Lord as the rivers of water; He turneth it whithersoever He will."

Proverbs 21:1 KJV

I do not go in my own way, dear Father,
  for I submit my will unto thee.
I will not choose the path to be taken,
  but I ask You to choose for me.
There are many paths; there are many ways to follow.
  I do not know which road I should take.
I desire to take your road, my Father,
  I do not want to make a mistake.
O' dear God, for your sure intervention.
  Oh, in the night I do seek your face.
Oh, Father, I need clearer direction, oh, Lord,
  help me, Spirit, the right path to take.
Oh, Jesus, there is none like you.
  Oh, Father, there is none like you.
Sweet Spirit of God, you alone are my guide,
  Blessed Lord, there is none like you.
You are far more precious than silver.
  You are more wonderful to me than gold.
You are not to be compared with others, O Savior,
  Your face is too grand to behold.
Oh, sweet Spirit, keep guiding my footsteps.
  Holy Spirit, keep guiding my way.
I submit my life unto Jesus, my Savior,
  I submit my will and my way.

Praying God's word

You do have the mind of Christ and hold the thoughts, feelings and purposes of God's heart.

I Corinthians 2:16 AMP

The king's heart is like channels of water in the hand of the Lord; He turns it wherever He wishes.

Proverbs 21:1 NAS

Many are the plans in a man's heart, but it is the Lord's purpose that prevail.

Proverbs 19:21 AMP

The lot is cast into the lap, but the decision is wholly of the Lord (even the events that seem accidental are really ordered by Him.)

Proverbs 16:33 AMP

Father, I thank you that I have the mind of Christ, and I do hold the thoughts, feelings and purposes of God's heart. I thank you that my heart is in your hand like a waterbrook and you can turn it whithersoever way that you would. Even though there are plans in my mind, your Word says you direct our steps and make them sure. I thank you, Lord God, that the decision I make will be wholly of the Lord and that all circumstances will be ordered by You.

Fellowship is only as deep as our truthfulness.

"Search me, O God, and know my heart: try me, and know my thoughts; And see if there be any wicked way in me, and lead me in the way everlasting."

Psalm 139:23,24 KJV

Sometimes it is difficult to answer God when we know we have sinned.

Adam and Eve sinned. God said, "Adam, where are you?" (Do we suppose God truly did not know Adam's whereabouts? Of course, God knew. But God wants us to respond to Him out of our will -- not because He is all knowing.)

Then, God in his sweet mercy "covered" Adam and Eve after repentance. That is God's response to our sin when we confess our sin to Him! "Unto Adam also and to his wife did the Lord God make coats of skins, and clothed them." (Genesis 3:21 KJV) Instantly, God restored man and his wife to Himself, and protected him with clothing.

Cain sinned by killing his brother. God said to Cain, "Where is Abel your brother?" (Again, as if God did not know!) Cain replied, "Am I my brother's keeper?" Second chance to repent, God said, "What have you done? The voice of your brother's blood cries out to Me from the ground." God knew all the time what happened to Abel. But He wanted to give Cain a chance to confess his sin. Cain tried to hide his sin. RESULT: Cain became a fugitive and a vagabond.

Spiritual truth: Lying to God without repentance leads to separation from God. Lies separate. Where there is no truth, there is no fellowship. Fellowship goes as deep as the truth. This is true in relationships with people and relationship with God.

God still "covers" us with His mercy and love. He *wants* to cover us. The minute we come to him in truthfulness, He covers us. He clothes us in His righteousness. Not one of us is righteous.

Worthy of repeating, let our prayer be: "Search me, O God, and know my heart. Try me, and know my thoughts. See if there be any wicked way in me, and lead me in the way everlasting."

Nothing can stop God from loving you.

"For I am convinced that neither death, nor life, nor angels, nor principalities, nor things present, nor things to come, nor powers, nor height, nor depth, nor any other creature, will be able to separate us from the love of God, which is in Christ Jesus our Lord."

Romans 8:38, 39 KJ

You are His....
    so completely His.
Neither height, nor depth, nor things present nor to come...
    not even the past can take you out of the reach of His hand.
He will eternally hold your hand --
    through every valley ....
    o'er every mountain ...
    down each sidewalk ...
    up every path ....
He will be holding your hand.
                You are His.

Oh, the mercy of God

"The Lord is compassionate and gracious, slow to anger and full of mercy. He has not dealt with us according to our sins, nor rewarded us according to iniquities. For as high as the heavens are above the earth, so great is His lovingkindness..... And as far as the east is from the west, so far has He removed our transgressions."

Psalm 103: 8-12 KJV

You wish you could go back and clean up your "mess."

It has already been done.

God is compassionate and gracious, slow to anger, and full of mercy.

He has not dealt with us according to our sins nor rewarded us according to iniquities.

He has purged us as white as snow. We are as unspotted as a new day. Each day is a new way to express your love for Him.

Live today in harmony with Him. The past is exactly that....*past*! It is over. There is no room in today or your future for *past* data. Behold, He makes all things new.

Shall you believe what someone else says you are, or who His Word says you are?

Jesus said, "Rise up and walk." The crippled from birth rose up, and left his crippled way behind.

Jesus said, "Stand forth" which means stand up and come forward...come out of the past, and come away from that which is behind you.

Jesus said, "Stretch forth," so let go of your past, let go of any limits in your mind, and stretch forth to Him to be made whole. Stretch to become all He can enable you to be.

Jesus said, "Neither do I condemn you," so if He does not condemn you, why condemn yourself?

The Lord is compassionate and gracious, slow to anger, and full of mercy.

You are exempt.

"When they came to Capernaum, those who collected the two-drachma tax came to Peter and said, 'Does your teacher not pay the two-drachma tax?' He said, 'Yes.' And when he came into the house, Jesus spoke to him first, saying, 'What do you think, Simon? From whom do the kings of the earth collect customs or poll-tax, from their sons or from strangers?' When Peter said, 'From strangers,' Jesus said to him, 'Then the sons are exempt.' (Then Jesus sent Peter to pay the tax.)"

Matthew 17:24 NAS

We are not strangers to God, but in deed, his sons/daughters. We are therefore *exempt* from the tax (exempt from having to pay what we rightfully owe -- our share.) Why? Because our father is the King, and He does not tax us, make us pay, for we are His children and it is His plan, His desire, His will that we should not have to pay our share, our "taxes," because Jesus paid it for us. The debt we rightfully owe has been paid, once and for all!

We owe a lot for our sins. But we do not have to pay!

Think of the toll bridges in some states, as you pass along the highway, you must stop and pay. But God has already paid the tolls through Jesus. So our way is paid.

If IRS called you today and said, "We forgive you all your taxes for the last ten years," what would you say? "Oh, no. I *want* to pay my taxes."

The amount at Disneyworld to enter the gates is the same dollar amount for each person entering. If you are divorced, you do not have to pay more to get in. If you have had drugs in your past, you don't have to pay more to get in. The price is the same. But once paid, each person is free to ride every single ride in Disney. You don't go to Space Mountain and say, "Oh, I can't ride that one because I made a mistake 10 years ago." You are free to ride. Only you can decide to take that privilege. There are no punishments or shame or guilt tokens you have to pay. We are all the same once the price has been paid.

Our righteousness is in him, not in us. We are exempt because of Jesus.

Are you loving YOURSELF?

"He that loveth his brother abideth in the light, and there is none occasion of stumbling in him. But he that hateth his brother is in darkness, and walketh in darkness, and knoweth not whither he goeth, because that darkness hath blinded his eyes."

I John 2:10 KJV

This unforgiveness thing is big. Way big. The spellcheck on this program doesn't even recognize the word "unforgiveness." Oh my. I wonder if that's why we keep tripping over the same problems, over and over. Maybe we don't "recognize" it. You know, the same "type" problems, over and over. Unforgiveness blinds our eyes. If we can't see, we stumble around.

Maybe, just maybe, it's not even unforgiveness for our *brother* that blinds us.

The first and greatest commandment is to "love your neighbor as yourself." So maybe, just maybe, there are areas in our own lives for which we have not forgiven ourselves: failure in relationships (spouse, child, relative, neighbor), dishonesty, infidelity, or other sins/failures. Maybe we forgave someone else, but not ourselves. Maybe inability in forgiving OURSELVES is our problem; blinding our eyes, causing us to trip over the same problem over and over.

Look closely.

Walk in the light by loving yourself.

Father, if there is ANY area in my mind, life, or heart today that is causing me to trip over the same problem again and again, please reveal the deepest source of that to me, so that I can forgive, myself or others, and no longer let unforgiveness be a source of stumbling to me.

Forget not all His benefits.

"Bless the Lord, O my soul, and forget not ALL His benefits!"
Psalm 103:2 KJ

Discouragement came.
But, the word of God came, too.
The word of God (Psalm 103) says:
"Bless the Lord, O my soul, and forget not ALL His benefits!"
Don't lose sight of *all* His benefits! The price has been paid! He paid exactly the same price for:

.....our salvation
....our healing
....our peace of mind.

He didn't:

....partially save us
....or partially heal us
....or give us partial peace.

Receive all of His benefits. A precious price has, indeed, been paid. His very blood. His life.

Yes, discouragement came. But the word of God came, too.

The victory is ours. Total victory. Not partial victory. Total. Forget not *all* His benefits.

Because we do not hear it all the time, because we are not surrounded by those who speak God's word, it is sometimes easy to lose sight of His benefits. It is easy to lose sight of His word and His promises. It is easy to take on the world's mentality.

Faith comes by hearing. Read and speak God's word to yourself. Speak it out loud to yourself, then you are hearing it and reading it, receiving it in two venues.

"He was wounded for our transgressions. He was bruised for our iniquities. The chastisement of our peace was upon Him. And with His stripes we are healed." Isaiah 53:5 KJV

"Bless the Lord, O my soul, and all that is within me, bless His holy name. Bless the Lord, O my soul, and forget not all His benefits." KJV

Be encouraged.

"Do not let your heart be troubled."

John 14:1 NAS

There's not one single place in the word where the Lord ever tells us to "be *dis*couraged." Over and over again, we receive the message to "be *en*couraged."

Elijah's mantle was the "sign" (if you will) of the anointing (or the call) on his life. After a great victory in I Kings 19, we see Elijah very discouraged because he felt he was the only prophet left in the land. He felt alone. He felt that no one stood with him. So discouraged, that in fact in verse 13 he "wrapped his face in his mantle."

Elijah became discouraged crying out to God, "I must be the only one left!" But I like God's answer: I Kings 19:18 "Yet I have left me seven thousand in Israel, all the knees which have not bowed unto Baal." NAS

Yes, there are others who are totally devoted to God, and they may not be in your sight, but they are in God's.

He surely will bring the right friends across your path at the right time. God is with you, and you are not alone.

Ever disappointed in other Christians? Unfortunately, there will be those in whom we are disappointed, and there will be those *we* disappoint. So let us take heart, remembering:

> Because I love thy law, nothing shall offend me. Psalm 119:165 KJV
> With me, it is a very small thing that I should be judged of you or of man's judgement, for it is the Lord who judgeth me! I Cor. 4:3 KJV

And at times when the "church" has let you down?

> "I'd rather be a doorkeeper in the house of my God, than to dwell in the tents of the wicked." Psalm 84:10 KJV

Wrap your face in the mantle God has given you. Wrapping your face in the anointing in which He has called you will prevent you from seeing anything else.

Don't let your heart be troubled. Nothing else matters but loving God. In whom would you rather trust? It is better to put your trust in God than in men.

Wrap your face, and do not let your heart be troubled.

Don't grow weary.

> *"And let us not lose heart in doing good, for in due time we shall reap if we do not grow weary."*
>
> *Galatians 6:9 NAS*

I'm wondering if there are times when you have felt as I?
Rejected and wandering, with eyes upon the sky
to see a sign, to hear a voice, to know a change will come.
An eternity it seems to be until His will is done.
Today seems brighter, tomorrow grows dim, our faith begins to wane,
but then we think upon His word -- today, forever, the same.
"Christianity," now that's a word that holds so many ways.
How, just how, can it be called His walk? His will? His name?
So I whisper to myself, "I think I'll try a new, a better way.
This 'Christianity' has disappointed me day after day after day."
The moment the thought escaped my brain, I heard the Master say:
"But have *I* ever disappointed you?" I said to Him, "No way."
Instantly I knew He's with me walking by my side.
I had to find no strength in man, in no one to rely.
It's not "their" fault, and it's not mine. Continually I grow,
and each lesson is more precious. It's God we come to know.
So take His strength, His word, His power.
He is the healing touch.
Just keep on walking when you're tired.
He loves you, OH, so much!
Rest in Him and in His love. Wrap your face in your gifts and calling.
He walks beside you every step to keep you safe from falling.

You have a future and hope with God.

"For I know the plans I have for you, declares the Lord, plans to prosper you and not to harm you, plans to give you hope and a future."

Jeremiah 29:11 NIV

Sometimes it seems as though we are full vessels, our cups are overflowing with the calling in which we are walking. Then, God pours us into a new vessel....a pitcher perhaps! Change comes, and the cupful suddenly feels inadequate and insecure.

Every ounce of what was in that cup is still there; it is just in a bigger vessel, and we are challenged to have faith to fill-up our new vessel....to be more like Christ. That just takes time. Our goal in every deeper calling is to reflect the image of Christ. Each path may be totally different, but none the less, our hearts are to reflect the Master.

Allowing God to reveal Himself in new ways is good for us. How can God change us if we are never in situations that require change in our lives? The greater the situational change, the greater the possible "change" in our lives. And it is up to us, in every change, to follow after the Master in an even closer relationship. He alone is our hiding place, our shield, our savior. We may not always know or understand the exact path we are on, or else we would have no need for faith. And, faith is what pleases God the most.

The Father's thoughts of us are good, and never evil, to give us a future and hope.

Dear Father: That we would know Your love like never before....see You more clearly; follow You more nearly; love You more dearly.

Wilt thou be made whole?

"After this there was a feast of the Jews; and Jesus went up to Jerusalem. Now there is at Jerusalem by the sheep market a pool, which is called in the Hebrew tongue Bethesda, having five porches. In these lay a great multitude of impotent folk, of blind, halt, withered, waiting for the moving of the water. For an angel went down at a certain season into the pool, and troubled the water: whosoever then first after the troubling of the water stepped in was made whole of whatsoever disease he had. And a certain man was there, which had an infirmity thirty and eight years. When Jesus saw him lie, and knew that he had been now a long time in that case, He saith unto him, 'Wilt thou be made whole?' The impotent man answered him, 'Sir, I have no man, when the water is troubled, to put me into the pool: but while I am coming, another steppeth down before me.' Jesus saith unto him, 'Rise, take up thy bed, and walk.' And immediately the man was made whole, and took up his bed, and walked: and on the same day was the Sabbath."

John 5:1-9 KJV

Oh, the Master is here and He says, "Will you be made whole?" Is our immediate answer, "Yes, Lord."?

You have lain at the pool of Bethesda long enough. No one is coming to set you in the stirred waters, for Jesus Himself has come, and He says, "Take up thy pallet and walk."

You don't have to wait on anyone else. You don't have to expect someone else to "lift you." You can't even blame anyone for entering first, or for lack of friends or family to "tote" you to healing. The power is in your own legs co-joined with your own response to the words of the Master.

Will you be made whole? He, Jesus, is willing. When we take it upon ourselves as our own responsibility, and we respond to Jesus, healing comes. We are then enabled to walk in newness. It is His desire that we be made whole, but we must answer "yes" and not offer excuses for "getting in the pool."

What are reasons the lame, hurt, wounded would say no? Because no one would "help" him into the water. See the shift in focus? The lame man blamed someone else for his lack of healing. The lame man did not promptly say "yes" for he had been in that state for so long, he almost did not recognize the Master. He could only look about and blame others. He saw his need above being able to see the Master. This lame man judged his lack of healing on others to "help him into it."

There is a great multitude awaiting the moving of the waters and people to "help them into the pool." But the answer is already here: It is the Master. The Saviour only wants a reply to "will you be made whole?"

Just say "yes." No blaming. Just say "yes." For no man, no woman, no child, no religion can meet the deep, deep needs we all have.

Don't let the Saviour go unnoticed at your pool. He is there. No rituals. Just say "yes" and take up your pallet and walk.

Don't be like the lame man who relied on the sympathy and indulgence of his friends, relatives, neighbors, for healing. For the Master has come to *your* pool.

Look unto Jesus. Say "yes." Don't wait on someone else to rescue you. He has come personally to rescue us!

Father God: I know I cannot even be drawn to you without your being the One who draws. I ask you, holy God, to draw me to you; to open my eyes to the presence of the healer, the holy one, Jesus. Let me be aware of your desire to bring healing to me, and Father, I say "yes," for I have lain in this state long enough and far too long. I take up my pallet and walk, leaving behind at the pool of Bethesda, at the five porticoes, (five being the number of grace and mercy), my lameness which has caused me the inability to "walk" without pain and rise above my condition. I thank you for healing me. I look steadfastly in your eyes and not at my inability. Strengthen my spiritual legs as I walk for the first time, Lord, for I am totally dependent on your mercy. And you are a good father, giving good gifts to your children. In you my weakness is made strong. Thank you, Father.

Be refreshed.

"Come to Me all ye who are weary and heavy-laden, and I will give you rest."

Matthew 11:28 NAS

It is a time of refreshing for all who will come near.

Seek Him early while He may be found.

Come to the waters and drink freely; waters of refreshing for all who come.

Come. Drink.

Today, see if He will not hasten His word to perform it.

Pull aside today. Meditate on God's word, and be still.

Will you make time for Him today? He has things to tell you.

You are so valuable.

"Are not five sparrows sold for two cents? And yet not one of them is forgotten before God. Indeed, the very hairs of your head are all numbered. Do not fear; you are of more value than many sparrows."

Luke 12: 6,7 NAS

He has inscribed your name in the palm of His hands. Your name is always before His eyes.

So what if the storms rage and the winds toss? With Him, you can rest in peace.

You are precious to Him. He knew you before you were even born. He formed you in your mother's womb. You are not a mistake.

He calls you by name. He knows the numbers of hairs on your very head. If He knows when a sparrow falls to the earth, does He not see all your comings and goings?

Every new day brings new grace. Forget yesterday. Forget the past. Enjoy now....today....the "present"....your "gift" of life.

Draw near to Him, and He will draw near to you.

Remember His word is a lamp unto your feet, and a light unto your path. You may see only a few steps at a time, or perhaps the path is curvy and you cannot see around the next turn. But have no fear, for He is with you. He goes before you, and He is behind you. He is on each side.

The floods shall not overtake you, and the fires will not burn you. For you are His, and He is with you. With you! In you! For you! And if He is for you, who can be against you and prevail?

His thoughts of you are good and not of evil, to give you a future and a hope (as in Jeremiah 29:11) He is a good God. Expect good things.

I know His voice.

"My sheep hear my voice, and I know them, and they follow Me."

John 10:27 KJV

Don't listen to the voice of a stranger. Sometimes even the voice of a friend can be the wrong voice in which to listen.

His sheep know His voice. His voice is His Word. Listen intently and carefully for His voice, for His voice will set at peace the thoughts of your mind.

His voice is not loud and demanding, but gentle and kind, for the goodness of the Lord is what leads men to repentance. It is a still, small voice. Don't let the noise of the world drown out His voice.

He clearly wants to speak to you and give you guidance every day. Listen to Him. Listen to His word. As you read it, read it aloud, and listen with your ears. You are then receiving a double portion of His word as you speak *and* listen.

Lean not unto your own understanding. Lean on God's word. He is the trustworthy one in your life. Follow Him as you read His word, and you will know His voice.

This is the way.

> *"Whether you turn to the right or to the left, your ears will hear a voice behind you, saying, 'This is the way; walk in it.'"*
>
> *Isaiah 30:21 NIV*

Follow closely, and listen carefully. Remember to hear "Walk ye in it." You have not ever set out to be misguided, for you have sought God. Every step is an effort to love Him more. Yes, you may have made some wrong choices, but keep pursuing Him!

Remember, man looks on the outward appearance, but God is looking at your heart!

You are the object of His attention. God has loved you all your life. You have been hungering and thirsting after the things of God, and yes, learning all along the way.

What is man, that God is mindful of him? Man is God's heart, God's creation, made in God's image. He wants to see His love demonstrated through the lives of men, women and children. Perfect love. Healing love. Forgiving love.

So wait patiently until you hear, "This is the way. Walk ye in it." When you hear nothing, do nothing. Wait. Patiently.

His mercy is new every single morning.

"The steadfast love of the LORD never ceases, his mercies never come to an end; they are new every morning; great is thy faithfulness. 'The LORD is my portion,' says my soul, 'therefore I will hope in him.'"
Lamentations 3:22-24 ESV

There are only a few brief moments of each morning that you can witness the splendor of the day as it awakens. It is filled with color -- hues of pink, yellow, blue and startling white.

Don't miss special moments with the Father. When you feel the unction, the tugging to set aside a few moments, do it. Don't be distracted by the demands of a day or the sounds of loud voices.

Pull aside.

Let God have a few moments. Share the splendor with your Father. These moments will be a constant reminder, a photo in your mind, for your whole day. Let God share moments with you.

He longs for you. No one can take your place. There is no one like you, for you were individually created for God. Some think they were created for others, but each person is created for God, that He might fellowship with each one individually.

The Father longs for your companionship. He wants to share His love with you.

His mercies and love are new every morning. He wants to bring you new hope every day.

He is your portion. Hope in God.

Let God have His way.

"And the peace of God, which surpasses all comprehension, shall guard your hearts and your mind in Christ Jesus."

Philippians 4:7 NAS

Follow the spirit. Don't lead. Wait.

Don't take matters into your own hands.

If it hurts you, it hurts others. If you hurt others, it hurts you.

You cannot ease others' pain by filling in for God. Let God have His way. He ultimately will, but the journey is better as you follow. You can not be a good leader if you are not following the Spirit of God.

Follow. Don't jump ahead.

When you lead, you lead self and others off. Follow God. Don't be afraid to back off.

Do nothing if God is not your lead man.

When in doubt, don't.

Don't guess at God's will.

Don't have your own way.

Efforts to rescue others will merely imprison you if God has not personally directed you.

If you follow God, He can protect your heart. He is not a selfish, strong-armed God. He wants us to *follow* so He can walk ahead to *protect.*

Trust Him with all your heart.

"Trust in the Lord with all your heart and do not lean on your own understanding. In all your ways acknowledge Him and He will make your paths straight."

Proverbs 3:5 NAS

Timing. It is God's. He will still clean up the mess, heal and restore hearts....the greatest miracle of all.

He can and He will.

Your tendency may be to SEE a glimpse and jump in full force to rescue or make it your will. Don't do it.

God gave instructions and every detail for the sanctuary. He did not love His hand-made sanctuary more than He loves you, your life, or the lives or others. For you *are* His sanctuary now, and He has every detail planned. How much *more* important are the details of your life than the details of the sanctuary?

Don't build with your own materials. He will provide them. See the glimpse. Enjoy. And then wait for Him!

Inquire each time you have a question. Each day has instructions. Listen and obey. Listen for God's instruction.

Let understanding come as a state of your heart, your being, though it may not be understood in your mind. Peace. You will know by peace.

Trust Him with all your heart. Acknowledge Him in every situation.

He is mindful of us.

"As far as the east is from the west, so far has He removed our transgressions from us. Just as a father has compassion on his children, so the Lord has compassion on those who fear Him. For He Himself knows our frame: He is mindful that we are but dust."

Psalms 103:11-14 NAS

It's just like falling down in a mud hole. Filthy. Sin just makes you filthy.

So you go take a shower. And the filth begins to wash off, dropping down into the shower drain, little by little, until there is not trace of the mud left. Maybe you stayed in the mud an hour, a day, a week, maybe years. But one good shower, and it is gone.

That's what forgiveness is like. We are cleansed by the washing of the water of the Word. We are cleansed because we ask for forgiveness. It doesn't matter if it was one day or one lifetime. Once we truly repent, ask God for forgiveness, and turn from our sin, our filthiness is cleansed by His love and the washing of the water of the word.

His word says, "As far as the east is from the west, so far has He removed our transgressions." He just doesn't remember our sin. God's forgiveness is like that.

I can just hear Him now if I were to *again* ask forgiveness about a sin I repented of ten years ago and left behind. I can just hear Him saying: "You did *what*?" *As far as the east is from the west!*

There's a reason He didn't say as far as the North is from the South. That is a measured distance from the North Pole to the South Pole. But there is no measuring the east from the west. It just never ends. You cannot find a beginning or an ending place for His forgiveness!

He is mindful of us!

Wisdom

"Blessed is the man who finds wisdom and the man who gains understanding. For her profit is better than the profit of silver and her gain better than fine gold. She is more precious than jewels; and nothing you desire compares with her."

Proverbs 3:13,14,15 NAS

"Long life is in her right hand. In her left hand are riches and honor. Her ways are pleasant ways and all her paths are peace. She is a tree of life to those who take hold of her, and happy are all who hold fast."

Proverbs 3:16,17,18 NAS

Father, I thank you for wisdom from your Word that it:

preserves me,
promotes me,
keeps me,
brings honor to Thee,
gives grace to my head,
gives me a crown of glory,
adds years to my life,
makes me happy,
is better than gold,
is more precious than rubies,
gives me length of days,
gives me riches and honor,
is pleasant,
is peaceful, and all her ways are peace,
is a tree of life,
is life to my soul,
is grace to my neck,
is a safe way,
is a stumble-free path,
is freedom from fear when I rest or sleep.

He is loving for a thousand generations.

"I lavish unfailing love for a thousand generations on those who love me and obey my commands."

Exodus. 20:6 NLT

Father:

Thank you for this particular promise, that you "lavish unfailing love for a thousand generations on those who love and obey" You. I humbly thank you for the one who was before me who loved You so, that You are lavishing me with your love now. And for a thousand generations after me, I thank you for the love you are lavishing on my present loved ones and your promised lavishing love on generations to come!

For my grandchildren:

As you hid the baby Moses from all dangers, hide my grandchildren from all dangers. Hide them in the secret place of your waters. Let no evil come near them. Let the word of God be heard and lived before their ears and eyes. Let them hear your voice at a very young age as did Samuel.

For my children:

Father: That you would be as the balm of Gilead healing every exposed and raw emotion and turning their thoughts into the very mind of Christ. Enlighten them in your love. Be their Father in the greatest sense of the word, showering them with your wisdom and favor. Let them be like You, Lord. Give them a heart of flesh to seek and know you, thirsting after you all the days of their lives.

My daughters-in-law:

I place them in your hands, Lord, that you would mold them, hold them, love them, and let pure love embrace them. Let them be a living incense of your presence to their husbands and their children, and to You. Capture their hearts, Lord. And let them be blessed as Ruth!

For sons-in-law:

Let them be love and peace to our daughters; walking in wisdom; loving our daughters like Christ loves the church; willing to lay down their lives to care for and love their wives. Let everything their hand touches prosper as they provide for their families. Let them hear You, and know You, and follow You.

For all of my family and extended families:

Let us all have a Mary spirit that we may sit at your feet from time to time, and not rush about in daily affairs, never forgetting that you are present and desiring our fellowship. Let us know You -- not know about -- but know You! Thank you for lavishing us with your love.

Your love is overwhelming us.

Thank you, Father, for your promises.

Gather manna every day.

"Blessed be the Lord, who daily loadeth us with benefits, even the God of our salvation. Selah"

Psalms 68:19 KJV

He daily loads us with benefits. His holy word (the Bible) loads us with great benefits.

The Word is like manna. It must be eaten daily, for what I gathered yesterday was for yesterday and today I need fresh manna. In Exodus 16, we read where God provided manna (daily bread) for his children while they were traveling to the promised land, and as we travel our journeys, there is daily manna for us, too, through reading His word. It is new every morning, and loads us with benefits.

Open my eyes, ears and heart, Lord to see, hear and know.

Thank you, Father, that you daily load us with benefits if we will only take time to gather your manna! Give me such a hunger for your word that I would not think of missing a "meal" or the "gathering" of one day's manna.

Walk steadily and slowly.

"The wisdom that is from above is first pure, then peaceable, gentle, and easy to be intreated, full of mercy and good fruits, without partiality and without hypocrisy."

James 3:17 KJV

To be a Mary: He sees your desire. You are happiest at His feet, and He is providing that for you. Just walk slowly. Sit quietly.

Make no efforts on your own to busy yourself at this time. All things are on hold. You are well taken care of. Provision has been made. Can you trust? He has never failed you yet, and He will not fail you now.

Do not be lead around by others. He is your divine guidance. Let no one else be your Holy Spirit.

There are certain things He must tell you as you are ready. Today He tells you one thing: Wisdom from above is pure, peaceable, easy to be entreated, providing you with the truth for the next step. And with each step taken, another is revealed for the next step.

And as you walk, God is with you, forging ahead. All you must do is walk steadily and slowly. Surely.

For surely the goodness of the Lord precedes and follows you all the days of your life. Why?

Because you are *His*, and He is yours, as Solomon Songs says, "I'm my beloved's and He is mine." What wouldn't one do for His "beloved"?

Just seek Him, for the wisdom of God is pure, peaceable, gentle, easy to receive, and full of mercy.

You belong to God.

"I am my beloved's and my beloved is mine."
Solomon's Song 6:3 KJV

There is no reason, no way to earn, this great love from the Father. We are His, and He is ours.

He lavishes us in His love, His mercy, His grace. Unconditionally.

The Lord is gracious, slow to anger, full of mercy. He has not dealt with us according to our sins.

He wants from us "relationship" -- our fellowship with Him.

Oh, how He loves us.

I am my beloved's and He is mine!

He is holding you with His right hand.

Even if someone else's hand may have hurt you, don't be afraid to take God's right hand. If someone's hands have withheld love and blessing from you, reach for God's right hand. If someone you greatly love is no longer there to hold your hand, His right hand is there for you.

Take His right hand.

> *"His right hand and His holy arm have gained the victory for you."*
> *Psalm 98:1 NAS*

> *"Your right hand, O Lord, is majestic in power, Your right hand, O Lord, shatters the enemy."*
> *Ex 15:6 NAS*

> *"Because He is at my right hand, I will not be shaken."*
> *Ps 16:8 NAS*

> *"In Your right hand, there are pleasures forever."*
> *Ps 16:11 NAS*

> *"Your right hand upholds me, and Your gentleness makes me great."*
> *Ps 18:35 NAS*

> *"Now, I know that the Lord saves His anointed; He will answer him from His holy heaven with the saving strength of His right hand."*
> *Ps 20:6 NAS*

> *"My soul clings to You. Your right hand upholds me."*
> *Ps 63:8 NAS*

"You have taken hold of my right hand."

Ps 73: 23b NAS

Dear Precious Father:
Just like a little child crossing a street, I reach for your right hand. And when I won't, or when I don't, I ask you to reach with your right hand for my hand. I want to trust you and walk hand-in-hand with you. I want to be safe with you. Thank you, Father, for your strong right hand.

Expose my heart to your light.

"Even the darkness is not dark to You, and the night is as bright as the day. Darkness and light are alike to You."

Psalm 139:12 NAS

Father,

When I think about the darkness of the most remote places of my heart, I know it is not dark to you. I know that You desire to expose every area of my heart to light. For once light comes to darkness, it is no longer dark, but becomes a pathway to a new place for me.

So, Lord, shine your light on any dark places in my heart. I surrender all. I want your greatest glory to be revealed in Me, so that I will know how to love You and how to love others.

In You there is no darkness. I invite You to work in me so that I, too, can know brightness in my soul.

Keep God's word in front of your eyes.

"Let your eyes look directly ahead. And let your gaze be fixed straight in front of you."

Proverbs 4:25 NAS

Give attention to My words.
Incline your ear to my sayings.
Do not let them depart from your sight;
Keep them in the midst of your heart.
For they are life unto those who find them and health to all their body.
Watch over your heart with all diligence, for from it flow the springs of life.
Put away from you a deceitful mouth and put devious speech far from you.
Let your eyes look directly ahead and let your gaze be fixed straight in front of you.
Watch the path of your feet and all your ways will be established.
Do not turn to the right nor the left;
Turn your foot from evil.

Proverbs 4:20-27 NAS

Read it again. Focus only on God's Word. Worthy of reading again...and again.

Having been with Jesus....

"Now as they observed the confidence of Peter and John, and understood that they were uneducated and untrained men, they were marveling and began to recognize them as having been with Jesus."

Acts 4:13 NAS

Peter and John were ordinary men with no special training, but they were recognized as men **who had been with Jesus**.

Oh, that others would see the evidence of our having been with Him, actually recognizing us as "having been with Jesus." Selah.

Like Moses, Father, make our countenance glow. Turn our hair white if you must, but let us see your glory.

Oh, Father, regardless of my level of education or training, I pray that your presence so illuminates my countenance, that people would not only recognize that I have been in your presence, but that my heart and mind would be daily changed because of your presence.

He is the great grief-bearer.

"Surely He has borne your grief and carried your sorrows. Yet you did esteem Him stricken and smitten of God, and afflicted. But He was wounded for our transgressions, bruised for our iniquities, the chastisement of our peace was upon Him, and with His stripes you are healed."

Isaiah 53:5 KJV

Don't hold on to grief. *Surely* He has born your grief.

Is He not your Father and He cares affectionately for you? Give your grief into His hand. Lean your head on His shoulder. He will lift the heaviness from you if only you can allow Him. His hands are capable, trustworthy, nail-scarred.

Cling to Him and never hold on to any troubles. Don't try to solve things by yourself. Give your grief to the Father. When you give Him your cares, He is free to work them out.

Always turn to Him first, before you look anywhere else. His love will lighten your path, one step at a time.

He, Jesus, has already paid the price for that grief. He *bore* it. So don't you *bear* it. *Surely* He has borne your grief and carried your sorrows. *Surely*!

If you are carrying grief, you carry it needlessly. Even the grief of regrets of the past. He is the great grief-bearer. He wants to carry your grief.

Surely.
He.
Has.
Borne.
My.
Grief.

Psalms 18 excerpts from "The Message"

"God, you are my castle.
I live in you.
You alone make me strong
You are bedrock under my feet.

"My God, the high crag....
where I run for life.
My cry brings me right into your presence.

"God reached all the way down
from the sky to the sea.
He pulled me out of that ocean of hate,
that enemy chaos --
there they hit me when I was down.
But God stuck by me!
He stood me UP on an open-field.

"God made my life complete
when I placed all the pieces before Him.
He gave me a fresh start.

"I am alert to God's ways.
I'm watching my steps
God rewrote the text of my life
when I opened the book of my heart to His eyes.

"The good people taste your goodness.
The whole people taste your health.
The true people taste your truth
The bad ones can't figure you out.
I take the side of the down-and-out
But the stuck-up you take down a peg.

"Suddenly, God, you floodlight my life.
I'm blazing with glory, God's glory.

"Everyone who runs toward God makes it!"

God is up to something eternal.

"For our light affliction, which is but for a moment, is working for us a far more exceeding and eternal weight of glory, while we do not look at the things which are seen, but at the things which are not seen. For the things which are seen are temporary, but the things which are not seen are eternal."

II Corinthians 4:17-18 NKJ

So, something didn't turn out like you planned? Things didn't turn out like you thought they might?

Always know God is up to something bigger and better; something eternal! He is working on our behalf.

We cannot judge by what we "see." Our job is to trust God. His job is to work things out for our well-being. Our job is to have Hebrews 11 kind of faith, and let God do what is good for our eternal well-being.

We can trust Him.

"When my spirit grows faint within me, it is You who knows my way."

Psalm 142:3 NIV

Don't worry about the "temporary." This too shall pass.

Set your eyes on the eternal.

The touchable Lord

"One of the Pharisees was requesting Him to dine with him, and He entered the Pharisee's house and reclined at the table. And there was a woman in the city who was a sinner; and when she learned that He was reclining at the table in the Pharisee's house, she brought an alabaster vial of perfume, and standing behind Him at His feet, weeping, she began to wet His feet with her tears, and kept wiping them with the hair of her head, and kissing His feet and anointing them with the perfume. Now when the Pharisee who invited Him saw this, he said to himself, "If this man were a prophet, He would know who and what sort of person this woman is who is touching Him, that she is a sinner."

Luke 7:36 NAS

Touchable Lord, I magnify you. I worship and adore you, and ask that my tears anoint your feet. I pray that my love and praise for you be as the alabaster vial of perfume, as a sweet incense to your nostrils. You recognize me. You know me. Yet you allow me to touch you and to sit in your presence. I thank you.

Even the disapproval of men, even the disapproval of religious people and the opinions of others cannot prevent you from demonstrating your love and forgiveness to me.

Oh, Father, I owe you so much, far more than most, for you have forgiven all my sin, all my transgressions, all my debt, and all my weaknesses.

All I owe: You paid it.

Ah, Lord, it is easy to love You more, for You have forgiven me more than a thousand sinners. You have forgiven my sin, and written in the dust so that they walk away one by one. For You have spoken.

Thank you, touchable Lord.

Oh, He has good plans for you!

"Eye hath not seen, nor ear heard, neither have entered in the heart of man the things that God has prepared for them that love Him."

I Corinthians 2:9 KJV

Let God choose. He sees from a panoramic view, and we can only see with our limited vision --- mere human eyes.

His eyes go to and fro over the whole earth. He sees all. He knows all.

Don't choose by yourself or FOR yourself.

If choosing, choose the good part....to sit at His feet and learn.

We cannot with our mere eyes even imagine the good things God has planned for us!

Be a wise giver.

"And the foolish said to the wise, 'Give us some of your oil, for our lamps are going out.' But the wise answered, 'No lest there should not be enough for us and you; but go rather to those who sell and buy for yourselves.'"

Matthew 25:8 NKJV

Give wisely, for giving to the foolish cannot help them....or you. To some, we should give our coat, or the shirt off our back, or water, or a meal, or our time.

But sometimes, wisdom means saying no. And that can be a very hard thing to do.

Pause, and think of this.

Dear Father:

I need wisdom to know when to give and when not, for it is my propensity to give until I give foolishly, and until I begin to resent giving, for sometimes, I give foolishly when it actually may hurt those to whom I am giving, not giving them a chance to come to their own ends where they may find you. Thank you for wisdom, Lord.

Keep listening for the voice of God.

"I will send you to Jesse...for I have selected a king for Myself among his sons."

I Samuel 16: 1b NAS

God told Samuel to "Fill your horn with oil, and go: I will send you to Jesse the Bethlehemite, for I have selected a king for Myself among his sons." I Samuel 16:1 NAS

When Samuel saw Eliab, he thought "Surely the Lord's anointed is before Him. But the Lord said to Samuel, 'Do not look at his appearance or at the height of his stature, because I have rejected him; for God sees not as man sees, for man looks at the outward appearance, but the Lord looks at the heart." I Samuel 16:6,7 NAS

Then other sons, possible selections, came before Samuel, each one being a possibility for the perfect will of God: Abinadab; then Shammah. Surely looked good, like maybe it was the will of God.

Jesse made seven of his sons pass before Samuel, but the Lord chose none of them.

Keep listening.

It may not be the first selection that comes to you that is the will of God.

Keep listening.

It may not be the second, or the third selection. God will confirm His choice.

Don't necessarily take the thing that looks "good in appearance" first.

Keep listening.

Father, help me to keep listening and not jump to conclusions. Help me to wait on Your perfect will.

As you love others, you love Me.

"And whoever in the name of a disciple gives to one of these little ones even a cup of cold water to drink, truly I say to you he shall not lose his reward."

Matthew 10:42 NAS

Oh, the love of God that flows through you
as you hold His Word in your hand,
always beholding your Father's voice
and not listening to the voice of man.

Obeying Him as He gently speaks,
desiring to please your Lord,
Oh, what pleasure you give to Him.
bathed and dressed in His word.

Keep listening, my child, for you've yet to see
the fullness of how it shall be.
The hearts and lives of broken men
are changed as you obey Him.

Aha! Don't you look on the sides of the road
or ditches and traps there will be.
Keep your eyes on me fastened
and your face straight ahead!
Press on for the mark to see Him.

Such joy you have given to your Father above.
Oh, how He delights in you.
When you minister love to others.
You minister love to Him, too.

Journal as you study God's word.

"Write all the words which I have spoken to you in a book."
Jeremiah 30:2 KJV

When God speaks to man, whether through the Word or in our hearts by faith, it is worthy of recording, so we don't lose sight of it. Not only is it worthy, it is important that we continue to keep His word before us.

The authors of the Bible recorded that which the Lord inspired. Now, today, 2000 years later, we benefit from the hand-recorded word of the Lord.

David, through the Psalms, recorded his victories, defeats, pain, suffering, joys, jubilations, and even worship. Today the Psalms bring us refreshment and encouragement from the Lord as we read them.

Even so, our recordings can be inspirational. So write. Write down your "messages" and intimate moments with God. Record His word to you.

Perhaps there is a scripture that comes alive as you read it. Record it. And record your thoughts as you write.

I encourage *you*, too, to record your fellowship with the Father. It can be a source of inspiration to you and yours for years to come.

Last thoughts from other inspired writers.

The next two "writings" are words of inspiration as recorded by others. They encouraged me and I offer them as encouragement to you to do your own daily journaling, too!

Different styles. Different messages. God speaks individually to each person. Each of the following writings gave me a message and encouragement. Each journaler has her own style.

Read the holy word of God (The Bible) and let His word speak individually to you. Record your own inspiration.

I know you will enjoy these journalings through these women of my family, and I hope you will be encouraged to read God's word daily and begin your own journalings!

God changed Rahab's life and He can change anyone's.

"Then Joshua the son of Nun sent two men as spies...saying, 'Go, view...Jericho.' So they went and came into the house of a harlot whose name was Rahab, and lodged there.....And it was told the king of Jericho....But the woman had taken the two men (the spies) and hidden them....She had brought them up to the roof and hid them in the stalks of flax which she had laid...and said to them (the spies) 'I know that the Lord has given you the land, and that the terror of you has fallen on us, and that all the inhabitants of the land have melted away before you. For we have heard how the Lord dried up the water of the Red Sea before you when you came out of Egypt, and what you did....And when we heard it, our hearts melted....for the Lord your God, He is God in heaven above and on earth beneath.'"

Joshua 2 (Shortened) NAS

I love the horrible, yuckiness being turned beautiful and redeemed... because that is all of us! How easy it is for us to be surprised by Rahab's "sudden faith." After all, she was a prostitute! (There I go, so just because she is a harlot she has no morals at all, there is no good to be expected?!) Not true with God!

Aha! But there was so much more to it! She believed! She didn't just take this opportunity to save herself and family from inevitable defeat in the natural, but because of her "confession" there was a spiritual awakening, redemption...salvation that would be eternal for her and her whole family! She looked at the arrival of the spies as her opportunity --- and she took it! God was literally knocking on her door!

Understanding that sin is sin, God encourages me so much by including Rahab in His word because He can use us ALL no matter our condition.

I love that our Father uses the least likely! More than that, I am always reminded that I can either exhaust myself in trying to *improve* me or realize God's grace is sufficient, and He can redeem the horrible and yuckiness of my life, any life!

2 Corinthians 12:9: And He has said to me, "My grace is sufficient for you, for power is perfected in weakness. Most gladly therefore, I will rather boast about my weaknesses, that the power of Christ may dwell in me." NAS

I am so thankful that when I fail or make a mistake it is just another opportunity to receive grace that only He can bestow, keeping me humble for when I get caught up in pride, I forget the need for grace. And a step further -- I never want to run out of grace for those around me for we are all sinners made righteous not by anything we do but truly only by His awesome never ending grace!

Whew!

by: Misty Magers Townsend

Go and cry.

"Moreover the word of the Lord came to me saying, 'Go and cry in the hearing of Jerusalem, saying 'Thus says the Lord...'"

Jeremiah 2:2

My first thought was, "When was the last time that I heard the word of the Lord?" Hence, I express my conviction and struggle for not making time with God *first*. Our purpose is to hear from Him and truly seek with all of our heart, soul, and mind His purpose.

A "*wow*" moment, was to hear the Lord command Jeremiah to "Go and cry." This is *bold*. He did not just send Jeremiah into Judah to say a few things to a few people. He sent Jeremiah into Judah to *cry* to them with passion and conviction to impress upon them to turn their focus from material things, pleasing people, and exalting their own abilities, back to the Lord's purpose. There is no lasting security apart from God. The action of "cry" as commanded by God to Jeremiah, in my perspective, is a serious expression of desperation and heartache.

I think of my eight-month old son. He is not able to speak, yet and in most cases, I believe that I have learned his nonverbal cues to help satisfy his needs. However, as every mom knows, there are many times his moan slowly starts to turn into a more passionate expressiveness because I am not figuring out how to satisfy the particular need. Within seconds, his face is completely red, and his voice has reached an octave that can probably be heard at Table Rock Mountain miles away in Walhalla. And he can go on like this for several minutes if I do not figure out what it is he wants. This cry, is desperation...persistent and determined, to get his point across with certainty and decisiveness, with the utmost confidence that it will help him achieve receiving an answer to his discomfort.

Do we ever get this way over what it is the Lord is commanding us to do? This level of passion and boldness speaks to me and encourages me to be more radical in my faith and purpose for Jesus Christ. I believe the Lord requires of us to "Go and cry" out to those who need Him.

by Keri Holder Unsworth

Last thoughts from the pen holder of And I call Him...."Father":

This is my life message: Hear Him yourself. He wants to fellowship with you. There is no one else who can take your place. His desire to be intimate with His people has never ever changed.

Remember in the Old Testament, He wanted to speak directly to His people, but they wanted a king. Thus, they chose leanness of soul --- they missed so many blessings by not taking "alone" time with Father God, by not seeking Him themselves, by wanting to hear from Him and about Him through others but not through their own seeking. It is a blessing to hear of God and His works through His servants, but it is a whole different level, fatness of soul, to hear Him yourself.

I have two sons. Neither can take the place of the other. The relationships with me are different because they have different personalities, but they are both equally important to me, for they are "mine," and no one else can take their places. And I long to love them, speak with them, and spend time with them individually. One son cannot take the place of the other. They are each flesh of my flesh, and bone of my bone, as we are God's, and I long to be with each one of them, together (corporately) and individually for some special one-to-one fellowship. I take great joy in hearing stories *about* their lives, but time *with* them is worth far more than good stories *about* them.

And that is how it is with our Father. He *l-o-n-g-s* to love us, speak to us, and spend time with us. Though I believe we have many different callings and purposes on earth, I do believe first and foremost, our purpose is for fellowship with the Father.

I believe He created us because He wanted fellowship. And He's so good, that once he created Adam, and saw that Adam was a perfect creation, He had compassion and gave Adam human fellowship, too. What a good and great God, to meet and recognize the need for fellowship. And because we are made in His image, He, too, must need and want fellowship!

He is longing for us....to fellowship with us. Just to sit with us for a cup of coffee to share time with us. He's so good. Because He longs to be in *our* presence, His very desire brings *His* Presence to us. Magnificent, Holy, precious, sweet presence.

Oh, I love Him.

Be a ready pen in the hand of your Maker. Let it flow freely as you write the whispers of your Father. Record what you hear, what you know, and let it refresh you in times to come.

Take the time to capture your own thoughts; your own writings; as He speaks to and inspires you, too, through His written and Holy Word.

Read, meditate, and write, for it will take you to deeper and higher places.

Besides you, Father, I desire nothing on earth.

OTHER THOUGHTS TO PONDER:

Submit to the good qualities of God, not to the bad qualities of man.

Pharaoh ridiculed Moses. Goliath ridiculed David. Crowds ridiculed Jesus.

As God gives us insight, we should completely obey -- not partially.

The natural inclination of the heart of man is away from God, though there is an innate longing for Him.

It is simple to come to the banquet of the Lord. Don't add your own rules.

Trusting God is like jumping off the counter as a child into your father's arms.

I love you.
Thank you for sharing this little book with me.

Father,
I desire nothing on earth as I desire you.
Thank you for seeing my heart
and for all the fellowship, the special moments,
we have shared
during this lifetime.
Thank you.

I Love you so,
Kitty

LaVergne, TN USA
01 October 2010
199334LV00002B/210/P

9 781615 072958